Stone City Blue

Ed Thomas

D1553362

Methuen Drama

Published by Methuen 2004

1 3 5 7 9 10 8 6 4 2

First published in 2004 by
Methuen Publishing Limited
215 Vauxhall Bridge Road
London SW1V 1EJ

Methuen Publishing Limited Reg. No. 3543167

A CIP catalogue record for this book is available
from the British Library

ISBN 0 413 77490 2

Typeset by Country Setting, Kingsdown, Kent
Printed and bound in Great Britain by
Bookmarque Ltd, Croydon, Surrey

Caution

All rights whatsoever in these plays are strictly reserved and
application for performance etc. should be made to the author's
representative The Rod Hall Agency Ltd, 3 Charlotte Mews,
London W1T 4DZ

No performance may be given unless a licence has been obtained

STONE CITY BLUE

BY ED THOMAS

Cast/Actorion

R1	NIA ROBERTS
R2	RYLAND TEIFI
R3	ALYS THOMAS
R4	RICHARD HARRINGTON

DIRECTOR	ED THOMAS
DESIGNER	MARK BAILEY
LIGHTING DESIGNER	JEANINE DAVIES
COMPOSER	JOHN HARDY
SOUND DESIGNER	MATTHEW WILLIAMS

COMPANY STAGE MANAGERS	ALISON SIÂN DAVIES
	MICHELLE JACKSON-MOGFORD

Clwyd Theatr Cymru
Thursday 21 October - Saturday 6 November
Dydd Iau 21 Hydref - Dydd Sadwrn 6 Tachwedd

The Riverfront, Newport
Thursday 11 - Saturday 13 November
Dydd Iau 11 - Dydd Sadwrn 13 Tachwedd

Chapter, Cardiff
(With the support of the Esmée Fairbairn Foundation)
Tuesday 16 - Saturday 27 November
Dydd Mawrth 16 - Dydd Sadwrn 27 Tachwedd

With thanks to the Stiwt Theatre, Wrexham and Llwyfan Gogledd Cymru.

CLWYD THEATR CYMRU

Created through the vision of Clwyd County Council and its Chief Executive Haydn Rees, Theatr Clwyd was opened in 1976. Located a mile from Mold town centre the building incorporates five performance venues: The Anthony Hopkins Theatre, Emlyn Williams Theatre, Studio 2, multi-function Clwyd Room for the community, Cinema and three art galleries.

Following Local Government Reorganisation in Wales, the theatre faced closure on 1st April 1997. The new Flintshire County Council and its Leader, Tom Middlehurst, asked Terry Hands to formulate an artistic and business plan to avert this threat and take the theatre forward .

Subsequently Terry accepted the post of Director on 2 May 1997 and asked Tim Baker to join him as Associate.

In 1998 the theatre won the Barclays/TMA Theatre of the Year award and in 1999 was designated a Welsh National Performing Arts Company by the Arts Council of Wales. The name was changed to Clwyd Theatr Cymru to reflect the theatre's new national remit and its new Welsh identity.

Clwyd Theatr Cymru is the home of a highly acclaimed producing company which also presents much of its work on tour throughout Wales.

Clwyd Theatr Cymru's 200 seat mobile theatre is a unique and innovative contribution to professional theatre touring within Wales. The production of **BRASSED OFF**, the fifth mobile theatre tour, was made possible by a £100,000 grant from the Welsh Assembly Government and sponsorship from LloydsTSB matched by equivalent funding from Arts & Business.

Forthcoming production in Mold: **TROILUS AND CRESSIDA** by William Shakespeare, directed by Terry Hands.

RICHARD HARRINGTON

Richard's theatre credits include: **Art & Guff** (Soho Theatre), **Unprotected Sex** (Sherman Theatre Cardiff), **Gas Station Angel** (Royal Court Tour), **House of America** (Tour/Fiction Factory), **Un Nos Ar Faes Peryddon** (Tour/Spectacle Theatre Co.), **Nothing to Pay** (Tin Language/Made in Wales), **The Snow Queen** (Sherman Theatre Co.)

Television work includes: **Dalziel and Pascoe, Silent Witness, Spooks, Gunpowder, Treason & Plot , Hustle , Rehab, Hidden City, Holby City, Fondue, Sex and Dinosaurs, Score, Care, Oh Little Town Of Bethlehem, Coronation Street, 31/12/99, Tiger Bay, Mind to Kill, Broken Glass, Civvies, 1996, Breeders, Iechyd da, The Proposition, Aeronaut, Oliver's Travels** and **Judas and the Gimp.**

Film credits include: **Joyrider, Mathilde, Secret Passage, Mule, House of America, Gadael Lenin, Dafydd** - for which he won Best Actor Award, Bafta Cymru.

Radio credits include: **Station Road** (BBC Radio Wales), **Night Must Fall** (Radio 4), **The Assasin** (Radio Drama Wales), **The Elizabethans** (Radio 4), **The Great Subterranean Adventure** (Radio 4), **A Civil War** (Radio 4), **Three O'Clock at Ponty** and **Baby Baby** (BBC Radio Wales).

Voice Work includes: **Scott Gibbs Documentary, Neil Jenkins - Working Class Hero, Falklands Stories** and **Human Traffic.**

NIA ROBERTS

Theatre Credits include: Imogen in **Cymbeline** at this year's Ludlow Festival, directed by Michael Bogdanov, **Under Milk Wood** (The Wales Theatre Company), **Past Away** (Sgript Cymru), **Cider with Rosie** (Theatr Gorllewin Morgannwg) and **The New Menoza** (Birmingham Rep).

Nia's television credits include: **Holby City**, three series of **Fondue, Sex and Dinosaurs, The Welsh in Shakespeare, Casualty, Sion a Sian, Outside the Rules, Doctor Terrible's House of Horrible, The Bill, The Wedding Party, Score, Border Cafe, A Light on the Hill, Dirty Work, In the Company of Strangers, Sunburn, Tattoo You, Y Palmant Aur, Halen yn y Gwaed** and **Newes of the Weeke.**

Film Credits: **Dal yma Nawr, Solomon and Gaenor** (nominated for an Oscar), **The Italian Canone Inverso, The Theory of Flight** and **Lois** (Best Actress BAFTA Cymru)

RYLAND TEIFI

Ryland is from Ffostrasol in Ceredigion.

Theatre includes: **Rape of the Fair Country**, **Hosts of Rebecca**, **Song of the Earth - the Alexander Cordell Trilogy**, **Under Milk Wood** (Clwyd Theatr Cymru), **Amazing Grace** (Peacock/Abbey Theatre Dublin), **Siwan** (Theatr y Mafodol), **Taliesin**, **Over the Stone**, **Lleuad yn Olau**, **Sgrech**, **Anna Mari lyfs Dic Wili** (Arad Goch), **James and the Giant Peach** (Sherman Theatre).

Television includes: **Fondue Rhyw Deinasors** for which he won the 2003 Bafta Cymru Best Actor Award, **Iechyd Da**, **The Bench**, **Y Stafell Ddirgel Treflan**, **Llafur Cariad**, **Y Palmant Aur**, **Halen n y Gwaed**, **Glan Hafren**.

Film includes: **Two Way Journey**, **A Penny for your Dreams**, **Lois**, **Y Cloc** and **Screen Gems**.

ALYS THOMAS

Alys trained at the Welsh College of Music and Drama and graduated in 1999.

Theatre includes: **Llyn y Fan Fach** (Cwmmi Mega), **Paradwys Waed** (Theatr Bara Caws), **Flora's War** (Clwyd Theatr Cymru).

Television credits include: **Sion a Sian**, **Xtra**, **Not Getting Any**, **Cracio**, **Dogma: Ali Meek Gets A Result**, **Score**, **The Slate**, **Running Away With The Hairdresser**.

Film credits include: **Arthur's Dyke**.

Radio work includes: **Shadow Of The Sickle** (BBC Radio 4).

ED THOMAS
DIRECTOR

Ed Thomas is a founder member of Fiction Factory where he has worked as a writer, director and producer since 1988.

Stone City Blue is his tenth play - others include **House of America**, **Flowers of the Dead Red Sea**, **Song From a Forgotten City**, **East from the Gantry** and **Gas Station Angel**.

His work has toured widely in the UK, Europe, Asia and the Americas and translated into eight languages. His work in theatre, television and film has earned numerous awards including BBC and Time Out Writer of the Year, three Celtic Film and Television Festival awards and BAFTA Cymru awards as a writer, director and producer for **Silent Village**, **Fallen Sons**, **House of America**, **Satellite City**, **Fondue, Sex and Dinosaurs** and **Dal:Yma/Nawr**.

He lives in Cardiff.

MARK BAILEY
DESIGNER

Mark Bailey has designed over one hundred productions in Britain, Europe and North America.

He is an Associate Artist of Clwyd Theatr Cymru where his many designs include: **Hobson's Choice, Brassed Off, Hay Fever, Waiting for Godot, One Flew Over the Cuckoo's Nest, Pleasure & Repentance, Portrait of the Artist as a Young Dog, Oleanna, A View From the Bridge, Blithe Spirit, Oh What a Lovely War, To Kill a Mockingbird, The Four Seasons, Silas Marner, Betrayal, The Rabbit, King Lear, Private Lives** and the Alexander Cordell Trilogy **(Rape of the Fair Country, Hosts of Rebecca** and **Song Of the Earth)**.

Other recent designs include: **Northanger Abbey** (Theatre Royal York), **Rat Pack Confidential** (West End, Nottingham Playhouse & tour),**The Resistible Rise of Arturo Ui** (Glasgow Citizens), **A Star Danced** (Watermill Newbury), **Melody on the Move** (English National Ballet), **The Threepenny Opera** (Royal National Theatre & Tour), **Double Indemnity, Ethel and Ernest**, Brian Friel's **Wonderful Tennessee** and Robert Lepage's **Polygraph** (Nottingham Playhouse).

Mark's work in Musical Theatre and Opera includes **Ariadne auf Naxos** (Maggio Musicale Florence and Opera de Lausanne), **Il Maestro di Capella, Susanna's Secret** and **The Telephone** (Buxton Festival), **Carmen** (ROH Linbury Studio), **Iolanthe** (D'Oyly Carte at the Savoy Theatre, London), **Ladders and Snakes** (Opera North), and **False Love/True Love** and **What Price Confidence?** (Almeida Opera). He has also designed The Watermill's **Fiddler on the Roof** which won the TMA Best Musical 2002 and **The Gondoliers** (also West End) which won the same Best Musical Production Award in 2001, **Ten Cents A Dance** (Watermill & Sherman Theatre, Cardiff), and **Babes in Arms** (New Theatre, Cardiff) as well as **Into The Woods** (Theatre Royal,York), **Cabaret** and **Irma La Douce** (Watermill Newbury) which were all nominees for Best Musical Production in the TMA/Barclays Awards.

Other productions in London include **The Importance of Being Earnest** (Old Vic & Toronto); **Entertaining Mr Sloane** (Greenwich & tour); **Peace in our Time** (Richmond); **A Judgement in Stone** (Lyric Hammersmith); **The Winslow Boy** (Gielgud) and **Present Laughter** (Aldwych & Wyndhams).

He also designed **Broken Lives**, a drama documentary for BBC 2's Year of the Family.

JEANINE DAVIES
LIGHTING DESIGNER

Jeanine's extensive lighting design credits include: **Angels Amongst the Trees, Polygraph, Wonderful Tennessee, The Boy Who Fell into a Book** (Nottingham Playhouse), **Macbeth** and **Measure for Measure** (Dundee Rep), **The Broken Heart** (RSC Pit), **Tom's Midnight Garden, Red, Red Shoes** and **Clockwork** (Unicorn tour/New York), **The Merchant of Venice** and **What the Butler Saw** (Crucible Sheffield), **A Christmas Carol** (Derby Playhouse), **Anna Karenina, Absurd Person Singular** and **Gasping** (Palace Watford), **Uncle Varick, The Breathing House** (TMA Award for Best New Play), **Death of a Salesman** and **A Madman Sings to the Moon** (Lyceum, Edinburgh), **Il Re Pastore** (ROH Linbury Studio), **Don Pasquali** (Scottish Opera Go Round), **Off Kilter** (Dance Base), **Rat Pack Confidential** (Nottingham Playhouse & Whitehall Theatre), **Lifeboat** (Tour/TMA Award Best Childrens' Show), **The BFG** (UK Tour), **POW** (Paines Plough), **The Woman Who Cooked Her Husband** (Number One tour) and **Zlatta's Diary** (Communicado Theatre Company).

JOHN HARDY
COMPOSER

John Hardy has written original music for over 140 television drama series and documentaries.

His working relationship with Ed Thomas began in 1992 with the adaptation of **Flowers Of The Dead Red Sea** into a chamber opera for Music Theatre Wales, which toured the UK and Germany. Other productions include **Song From A Forgotten City** and **Gas Station Angel** for the stage and the feature film **Rancid Aluminium.**

Highlights of John's career include winning a BAFTA Cymru award for scoring the Oscar nominated **Hedd Wyn, Ymadawiad Arthur,** directed by Marc Evans, and another BAFTA Cymru Best Original Music award for the series **Fondue, Sex and Dinosaurs.**

John has also made music for **A Clockwork Orange** and the 50th anniversary remake of **Under Milk Wood** for BBC Radio 4 .

MATTHEW WILLIAMS
SOUND DESIGNER

Matthew, known to everyone he works with as Wills, trained at Clwyd Theatr Cymru and the School of Sound Recording, Manchester.

Other shows for Clwyd Theatr Cymru that Matthew has designed sound for include: **The Cavalcaders, The Glass Menagerie, The Journey of Mary Kelly, Hosts of Rebecca, Of Mice and Men, Twelfth Night, Macbeth, Word for Word/Gair am Air, Damwain a Hap/Accidental Death of an Anarchist, Private Lives, The Secret, To Kill A Mockingbird, Dealer's Choice, Betrayal, Romeo and Juliet, Blithe Spirit, The Crucible, Silas Marner, Oleanna, Portrait of the Artist as a Young Dog** and **Hobson's Choice.**

In his spare time, Matthew also works from his home studio where he works for various artists and record labels. He was the engineer/co-producer of the 1997 CD release of 'Nocturnal Nomad' by Dogs D'Amour frontman,Tyla.

Matthew has continued to work closely with Tyla, mastering/ editing his last 7 releases for King Outlaw/Cargo Records, and various pre-mastering work on Antiproduct's new album, **Made in the USA** (featuring well known American guitarist, Alex Kane), and the new release by New Disease (featuring Mark Thwaite, ex The Mission/Tricky and also Rich Battersby, ex Wildehearts).

Matthew was also the engineer/co-producer of Clwyd Theatr Cymru's CD release of music from **The Alexander Cordell Trilogy.**

Stone City Blue

Characters

R1
R2
R3
R4

The playscript that follows was correct at the time of going to press, but may have changed during rehearsals.

R1 Winter in the city.

R2 Saturday night.

R3 Seven after midnight.

R4 I'm in a hotel room.

R1 An anonymous –

R2 Corporate –

R3 Functional –

R4 Double-bedded hotel room.

R1 With desk and chair.

R2 Built-in wardrobe.

R3 Small safe.

R4 Tea- and coffee-making facilities.

R1 Highland biscuits.

R2 Mini-bar.

R3 Telephone.

R4 TV with Internet access.

R1 En-suite bathroom with free soap, shampoo and conditioner.

R4 And I'm alone.

R1 With my demons.

R2 My angels.

R3 My naked succubae.

R4 Waiting.

R1 For a stranger.

R2 A perfect stranger.

R3 To knock on my door.

Beat.

R4 Who I am and where I come from nobody in this city knows.

R1 The name on the passport isn't mine and neither is the ring on my finger.

R2 Those who think they know me call me Ray.

R3 Crazy Ray.

R4 Where real Ray is only real Ray knows.

R2 You want to sit down, Ray?

R1 Come and sit down by here.

R2 No no, he can sit here.

R1 Where do you want to sit, Ray?

R2 He can sit here, there's no trouble.

R1 Ray?

R3 Sit down by here.

R1 Decisions, decisions, decisions, what you say, Ray? Where do you want to sit?

R3 Maybe you don't want to sit?

R2 Course he does, can't just stand there with us sitting can he?

R1 Come and sit here . . . Ray?

R3 He don't want to sit and if he don't want to sit then let him stand.

R2 Come on now, cut it out, you're confusing him, if Ray wants to sit he'll sit in his own time, won't you, Ray?

R1 All I'm saying is he can.

R3 Let him sit where he wants.

R2 Ray, you sit where you want . . . in your own time, make yourself at home.

R4   Home?

R2   What's ours is yours . . . Ray?

R4   This isn't home.

R1   No, but it's a temporary home.

R4   Is that the same thing?

R2   No, but it's all we can do for now.

R4   We?

R2   Yeah . . . we.

R4   Who's we?

R1   All of us.

R2   Me.

R1   And me.

R3   And me.

R2   And you.

R4   How come I'm a you not a me?

R2   You are a me.

R4   You just called me a you.

R2   I meant me.

R4   So why say you?

R2   It's just a turn of phrase, if you want to be a me say me.

R4   Me.

R2   Bingo, you're a me.

R1   Just like the rest of us.

R4   The rest of us?

R1   Four me's make an us.

R4   Right.

R1   Me.

R2   Me.

R3   Me and . . .

R4   Us.

R3   No, Ray, you say me there.

R4   Me there.

R2   You say just me.

R4   Just me.

R3   No, Ray . . . me. After we say me me me you say me. You got me?

R4   Yeah.

R1   Four me's make an us.

R4   Right.

R1   So say me.

R4   Me.

R1   Good.

R2   Me.

R3   Me.

R1   Me and . . .

R4   Me.

R2   Bingo.

R1   You got it, Ray.

R3   Now come and sit down here with us.

R4   Is that my chair?

R3   If you want it to be.

R1   Do you want it to be?

R4   I'm easy.

R2   So sit down.

R4   I will.

R1   So how've you been?

R4   I've been cruising the city.

R2   That's good.

R4   Seven in the night till seven in the morning, twelve hour shifts six nights a week forty-eight weeks a year.

R3   Sounds busy.

R4   It is. I've been working on the number twenty-four. Twelve hours I work, twelve hours I don't, I've been counting one to a thousand, then after every thousand I make a mark here on the floor, 3,600 seconds makes an hour, twenty-four times 3,600 makes 86,400. On the floor in front of me there are forty-three marks, that was at least four hundred seconds ago. Forty-three marks means twelve hours, so by my reckoning it's time to go back to work.

R1   You sure, Ray?

R4   I'm sure, I got no time to sit down, I got to go to work.

R3   Take care, Ray.

R4   I will.

Beat.

And most nights I do.

R3   Alice.

R2   Angela.

R1   Branwen.

R4   Caroline.

R3   Catherine.

R2   Charlotte.

R1   Clare.

R3   Diana.

R4   Elaine.

R3   Florence.

R2   Gwennyth.

R1   Hannah.

R4   Heather.

R1   Holly.

R2   Lily.

R3   Louisa.

R4   Maria.

R3   Nina.

R2   Pearl.

R1   Ruby.

R4   Sandra.

R3   Teresa.

R2   Wendy.

R3   And Yvonne.

Beat.

R4   I hug them all, I bathe them all with holy water. I make them clean.

R2   Caroline is always the hardest
Caroline is always . . . difficult
But she's a legend.
People come from far and wide
To pay homage in blood and bone and spit.

With salt and vinegar
And broken promises.

R4   I like it when it's just me and her.
When the night is nearly over I hug her tightly.
My brush against her kerb.
I make her clean.
The left side then the right.
Up and down.
And all over.
I leave her spotless . . . to face a new day.
In my cleaning trolley.

R2   One forward gear.

R1   One reverse.

R4   A water jet.

R2   Rotating brushes.

R3   A heater.

R4   Windscreen wipers.

R2   Portable radio-cassette.

R1   With batteries.

R3   My refuge from the storm.

R4   I'm the hugger of streets –

R1   The crawler of kerbs –

R2   In the city of women's names.

Beat.

R4   But tonight things are different.

R3   Because tonight's my night off.

R4   I'm free from crazy Ray and the people who think
they know him.
I am myself.

R2   Me.

R1   Myself.

R3   I.

R4   In a hotel room.

R2   Alone.

R4   But who am I?

R1   What am I?

R3   How did I get here?

R2   Am I still the man I used to be?

R4   Am I a drunk?

R1   A lapsed Christian.

R4   A failed poet?

R3   A whore?

R4   Why do you ask?

R2   Are you testing me?

R1   Not testing as such.
Just establishing a common ground, a common experience.

R2   Ah.

R1   Did you go to university?

R4   Yes.

R3   Which one?

R2   An unfashionable one.

R1   Where?

R4   A provincial city.

R2   Which city?

R4   Cardiff.

R1   Is it unfashionable?

R4 It was then.

R2 Do you think it is now?

R3 It's better now than it was then, yes. Then it was viewed by some as a kind of Siberia.

R2 Some, but not all?

R3 The fortunate ones who came from more fashionable cities and more comfortable families who for whatever reason whether it be booze or drugs, a combination of both, or were just plain thick, fucked up their exams and after long conversations with disappointed parents took a route through clearing on their last option and arrived in Siberia.

R2 Cardiff Siberia.

R3 As it was looked upon then, yes.

R4 But not now.

R3 Not in certain quarters, no, it depends who you believe.

R2 Who do you believe, in your opinion?

R1 Belief and opinion are two different things.

R2 In what way?

R4 You may have an opinion you don't believe in.

R2 Doesn't that make you dispassionate?

R4 Not necessarily, life has taught me to be wary.

R2 Very wise.

R4 I've been struck too many unexpected blows to behave any differently.

R2 The school of hard knocks.

R4 I might appear to you on the outside as a man who's quite hard, quite tough, but on the inside I can be like putty.

R1 That's a very honest thing to say.

R4   I'm an honest man.

R2   But wary.

R4   Honesty is not always the best policy. I've been described by some as being too sensitive, as a result I've reined myself in, exposed myself to fewer situations where that sensitivity might lead to my downfall. Now I try to avoid situations that break my heart, degrade and humiliate me or generally drive me insane.

R2   Would you care to elaborate?

R4   It depends on whether I trust you.

R2   Do you trust me?

R4   I don't know.

R1   I trust you.

R2   Really?

R1   There's something about your face, your eyes perhaps, that says don't worry, you can trust me, if you've got something you want to say, say it, no matter how painful that is.

R2   I'll take that as a compliment.

R1   Please do. After all, we all have secrets, things we keep inside ourselves that we should bring out into the open and explore.

R3   Letting them fester inside is unhealthy.

R1   Very.

R3   They can destroy you.

R1   Yes.

R3   Even drive you insane.

R1   Most definitely. And if you share those secrets with anyone you have to be sure that you trust them, that you won't be judged by them.
And for some strange reason I trust you.

Beat.

Does that make me a fool?

R2   No, I think I'm now a very trustworthy person, I've learnt the value of not betraying confidence.

R3   But you haven't always been.

R4   The man who hasn't suffered the pain of his own humiliation hasn't lived.

R1   In your opinion.

R2   It's an opinion I believe in, yes.

R3   Based on a personal experience.

R4   Yes.

R1   You're more passionate than I expected.

R2   I'm more trustworthy than you think.

R3   But wary.

R4   Yes.

R1   And sensitive.

R2   Like putty, sometimes the smallest things can cut me to the quick.

R4   Like the trouser press.

R1   The trouser press?

R2   If you notice, we left it out of the long and detailed description of the room.

R4   We left it out?

R2   I mean I did.

R1   I can't say I noticed it.

R4   It's between the mini-bar and the wardrobe.

R1   Ah.

R3   And it upsets you?

R2   It can do.

R3   That's why you deliberately left it out of the description of the room?

R4   Yes.

R2   But it's not the only thing you left out.

R4   Isn't it?

R1   No.

R2   You also left out the low-level WC and bidet.

R1   Yes.

R2   And the standard lamp.

R3   Yes.

R2   But perhaps most important of all, you never mentioned the Bible in the drawer and the handwritten note underneath it.

R4   What handwritten note?

R2   This handwritten note.

'One may have a blazing hearth in one's soul yet no one ever comes to sit by it. Passers by see only a wisp of smoke rising from the chimney and continue on their way.'
Sainte Beuve. Spelt S-A-I-N-T-E. The E's a dead giveaway.

Obviously French.

R4   He or a she?

R3   Hard to tell.

R4   Did Sainte Beuve write it down or was somebody just quoting something he or she had written before?

R2   Why go to the trouble?

R1   Isn't it just a fancy way of saying no one gives a fuck?

R2   Born alone.

R3   Die alone.

R2   Get on with it.

R1   No big deal?

R4   Maybe. (*Beat.*) So who wrote it?

R1   Could it be John?

R2   Who's John?

R1   Maybe he wrote it and put it in all the rooms under all the Bibles, like a promotion. Maybe Sainte Beuve is an unknown writer in a Parisian garret that John knows and wants to introduce to the world as a world-class writer.

R4   You call that world-class?

R2   Who's John?

R1   I'm only surmising.

R4   So how come I haven't heard of him?

R2   Because you know fuck all about literature.

R4   And you do?

R2   I went to university!

R4   So you say.

R3   I studied English.

R4   So.

R2   So I know about literature.

R4   And you call that world-class?

R2   Questions, questions, questions, will you quit bullying me?

R4   I'm not bullying you.

R3   You are.

R4   Am I?

R1   Yes.

R2   When you bully me I go into my shell.

R3   If he goes into his shell it's a bugger to get him out.

R2   If I don't get out I get depressed.

R1   If he gets depressed I get suicidal.

R4   When I'm suicidal I'm a bugger to be with.

R2   When he's a bugger to be with I feel alone.

R1   When you feel alone you get depressed.

R3   When I get depressed I turn to God.

R4   But because you're depressed God can't hear you.

R2   When God can't hear me I feel suicidal.

R1   When I feel suicidal the black dog inside me tells me to kill myself.

R3   If I kill myself he'll be alone.

R4   If I'm alone there's no one to protect me from being bullied.

R3   And when he's bullied he goes into his shell.

R2   And when I go into my shell it's a bugger to get me out.

Beat.

R3   It's a bastard.

R1   It is.
Trust me. I know him. I've lived with him, he scuttles between depression and suicide like a coked-up cricketer who's forgotten his bat. So go gentle on him . . . please.

R4   I stand corrected.

R1   Good.

R4   So who's John?

R1   Ah.

R3   Ah.

R2   Ah.

R1   John Malkovitch.

R3   He part-owns this hotel.

R2   The Big Sleep.

R4   I remember.

R2   It's not the reason I came here.

R3   I just like the name. And I needed a sleep.

R1   A Big Sleep.

R4   I think the receptionist was Russian.

R1   Business or pleasure, sir?

R4   Pleasure.

R2   What else could I say?

R4   And as she hands me the room key –

R1   Room 24 on the second floor –

R4   I notice his photograph on the wall, John Malkovitch, looking mysterious.

R3   I saw him being interviewed once. Came over as a nice bloke.

R2   Seen a few of his films.

R4   I've got nothing against him. Don't even know him. And he doesn't know me. It's not as if the Russian girl at reception called him up after I'd checked in and said –

R1   I'm sorry to bother you, Mr Malkovitch, but I thought you should know that Mr Jones checked in. Mr Ray Jones. He's in Room 24 on the second floor.

R4   And it's not as if he said –

R2   Thank you, Ludmilla, tell him I'll be down straight away.

R4   Because it didn't happen . . .

R3   Because nobody called.

R4   And I don't expect him to call. I mean, I'm not exactly waiting for him. Not me.
And even if he did, I'm not sure I'd answer anyway. I've come here to relax, not socialise, I've done enough socialising.

R1   Sometimes I'd go out on Tuesdays and not come back till Sunday.

R2   Once I ended up on the south side of the city in a pair of trousers that weren't mine.

R3   A small party.

R4   People said I didn't look too good and that I should eat.

R1   Chicken.

R4   I pushed it around the plate till they got so loved up and stoned they didn't notice.

R2   I sat on a settee. Just me and a Sinatra record going round and round.

R1   And then I saw this kid in pyjamas.

R3   Must have been about five, said he couldn't sleep.

R1   He stepped up on the settee and looked over the back.

R3   There's a river down there, he says.

R4   I look down at the blue carpet. You're right, I say. Fancy a fish?

R2   We fished till daybreak, me and the boy, pulling the strangest fish from the carpet you ever saw.

R1   Then the boy fell asleep.

R4   I let myself out.

R2   And I walked the streets.

R4   Counting fish.

R2   With a hole in my heart.

Beat.

R4   He could have been my son.

R1   I've always wanted a baby. Not a giant family. Just one. I think it would change my whole life. I don't think I'd be as selfish. Am I selfish? Am I?

R3   She thought she'd have one with you.

R4   I know.

R2   You were the love of her life.

R4   I was.

R2   But you turned out to be not the man she thought she knew.

R4   I am not the man I used to be.

R1   No.

R4   Who am I?

R3   What am I?

R2   How did I get here?

R4   I'm just a stray dog cruising the city.

R2   A lost dog hugging the streets.

R3   Looking for a scent.

R1   A trail.

R4   A path.

R3   A way.

R2   To be connected again.

R1   To be reborn.

R4   Free.

R2   To belong again.

R4   To forgive again.

R1   And be forgiven.

R3   To love.

R1   And be loved.

R4   Not hate.

R2   Or be hated.

R4   Not kill.

R1   Or be killed.

R2   To be home.

R1   Home.

R3   Home.

R4   Home is just a memory
I keep it inside me
Like the corpse of a still-born child
A womb for the dead.
Am I dead?

R1   Am I?

R3   Am I?

R2   That kitchen was my home. We were like a family in
there. We were like the UN.
Greeks, French, Somalis, Italian, Koreans . . . me.
It was high-class. Hoi-polloi, ribs, racks, rabbits, roasted,
grilled, flash-fried, pan-fried, fish, prawns, duck.
Busy it was. It was summer. There was a run on steaks and
fish. Piece of piss. Angelo was off sick. He takes the rubbish
out. That night I did it to help out. It was hot. I could hear

people coming out of the pubs and heading for the clubs on
St Mary Street and Womanby. Must have been about half
eleven. The skip trolley was in a quiet alley. I lit a fag and
looked at the sky. (*Beat.*)
Then I opened the lid and there amongst the rubbish I saw
a pair of beautiful brown eyes. Like glass staring back at me.
I left the kitchen not long after that. I kept on seeing that
face over and over again. Wouldn't leave me. A woman she
was. A dead woman, looking back at me. Like it was my
fault.

Beat.

R1   Who was the woman?

R2   I . . .

R3   Who was the woman?

R2   She was . . .

R4   Who the fuck was the woman?

R2   They said her name was Caroline.

R4   They said?

R2   I read it in the newspaper.

R4   Which newspaper?

R2   The one I found outside my door.

R1   The hotel room door?

R2   Yes . . . I needed to relax.

R3   Chill out.

R4   Recharge my batteries.

R2   Catch up on my sleep.

R1   John would understand that.

R4   If he knocked on my door.
And I said –

R3   I need to relax.

R4   He'd say –

R2   No problem, Ray, I understand.
You take it easy.

R4   It's been a busy time, I'd say
I need to think things through
Think clearly
When I've done that I'll feel better, see, John.
I'll look better
I'll be myself again
Won't feel so frazzled
Stressed
Strung out
You know what I'm saying, John?

R2   I know what you're saying, Ray.

R4   I'll be able to cope better
Better than I have been
It's been a difficult time.

R2   I can see.

R4   I've been gripped by inertia on the one hand and rage
on the other.

R2   Not a happy combination.

R4   No. (*Beat.*) To many I've recovered, my eyes are clear.
And in social situations I'm not as prone to the darkness that
used to grip my mind like a fever.

R1   But it's a lie.

R4   Yes, in truth I can't sleep, can't eat, can't love, can't
fuck, can't live in my own skin.

R1   In short I'm walking around my own life like a
stranger.

R4   Yes.

R3   Disconnected.

R4   Yes.

R1   A bag of bones with thoughts.

R4   Yes.

R3   Incoherent.

R4   Yes.

R1   Dark.

R4   Yes.

R3   Lost.

R4   Yes.

R1   A bum.

R4   Just a bum at the edge of my own story.

R1   So what's the story?

R4   People don't understand see, don't know what I've
gone through. Am still going through.
Don't know they've been born, some people.
Call themselves your friends then they stab you in the back.
They're cunts, John, cunts.

R3   Fuckheads.

R4   Fucking trouser-pressers.

R2   Trouser-pressers?

R4   Yes. Every time I see a trouser-press I think of them.

R2   Them?

R4   I'm a sensitive man see, John, sometimes the smallest
thing can affect me.

R1   Like the trouser-press.

R4   Yes.

R2   Strange.

R4   I know. Even though it's a twentieth-century relic,
a dinosaur and generally a piece of shit, it's not the design
itself I'm most sensitive to.

R2   Oh.

R4   My main argument is with the people who by and
large use it. And by that I don't mean the good guys, the
people who've travelled far with their suits stuffed into bags
and who that day have to go to a family do –

R1   Or a wedding or funeral –

R4   And to look decent have to use the trouser-press.
I'm not having a go at them. As far as I'm concerned under
those circumstances the trouser-press is perfectly acceptable.

R3   Horses for courses.

R4   Exactly. But the fact is they're few and far between.
The crumpled linen suit which I notice is getting more
popular every day is making those circumstances I've just
described more uncommon.
So it means that the good guys in linen are not going to get
caught short.
Which means that the trouser-press to them is redundant.
Not needed.

R1   A dinosaur.

R4   Which leads me to my point.
The only person currently requiring the trouser-press in the
twenty-first century is the businessman.

R3   The busy . . . ness . . . man.

R4   Or, as I'd like to call him, the businesscunt.

R1   Who wakes up in hotel rooms.

R4   Like these.

R3   All over the world.

R4   And the first thing he does is press his spunky trousers
in a useless fucking trouser press before slicking back his hair

then going out into the world to stitch some poor unsuspecting bastard up for good!

R1   Fuck him completely.

R4   Ruin him.

R1   Send him out to a hundred-mile desert waterless.

R4   Till the sun cooks him.

R3   Roasts him.

R4   BURNS HIM TO A FUCKING CRISP!

Beat.

Cunted by cufflink he is.

R1   Shafted by a shirt he is.

R4   Pissed on by trouser-pressers. Till his head's ironed flat.

R3   Flat.

R4   Flat. (*Beat.*) It's a fucking disgrace.

R2   I can see that you've given it a great deal of thought.

R4   I'm a sensitive man.

R3   Too sensitive.

R4   I can be like putty.

R1   It makes me very angry. It makes me want to run up to some poor fucker tumbling out of McDonald's or Miss Milly's or PERFECT FUCKING PIZZA and say –

R4   GET AWAY FROM THERE, YOU STUPID FUCKER. THOSE SICK MULTINATIONAL CUNTS ARE CONNING YOU, KILLING YOU! IT'S ALL CRAP, TOTAL CRAP! THEY'RE CONNING YOU BEHIND YOUR BACK, FUCKING YOUR WIFE WITHOUT YOU KNOWING, POISONING YOU, MAKING YOU A FOOL, MAKING A BAD TASTE IN YOUR MOUTH, PISSING ON YOU, THE ONLY THING YOU CAN DO IS WALK AWAY, SAY FUCK YOU TROUSER-PRESSING

CUNTS, YOU CAN'T FUCK WITH ME OR MY WIFE,
YOU FUCK WITH ME AGAIN AND I'LL KILL YOU,
YOU HEAR! DO YOU?

Beat.

And does the poor fucker listen? Does he? Do I hear him
howl? Do I hear him revolt?

R3   No.

R4   Nothing.

R1   Only silence.

R3   Submission.

R1   Chips and no choice and a paper hat for your baby.

R4   Conned.

R1   Cunted.

R3   Hopeless.

Beat.

R4   It's enough to drive a sensitive man to the bottle.

R2   I never thought –

R1   You couldn't imagine how many nights I've spent alone
raging against the powerful on behalf of the weak in the
darkness and alienation of my room, recording my thoughts,
trying to make sense of the senseless, find truth in the lies,
praying that one day you I and every living pitiful soul will
see through the crap . . . (*Beat.*) It's been a lonely journey . . .
fucking lonely . . . there've been times when . . . when I . . .
when . . . oh fuck it, what does it matter . . .

Beat.

I'm sorry, I didn't . . .

R2   No, no.

R1   Mean to . . .

R2 It's fine.

R1 I just . . .

R2 It's good to let off steam.

R1 I didn't want you to think . . .

R2 It's fine . . . honestly . . . trust me.

R1 Is it?

R2 Yes. It's obvious that your feelings are genuine. How you came to possess them only you know. But it's obvious to me that they come from strong and committed political belief. In these times of indifference and apathy it's to be applauded, even welcomed. These are difficult times, dangerous times, the problems we face need good people to overcome them, committed people, passionate people. People who don't mind standing up for what they believe in.

Beat.

People like you and, God knows, even people like me.

R4 But you're a Hollywood star, John.

R2 I know, but even for me life isn't easy.

Beat.

I got to go, Ray.

R4 You sure?

R2 Been nice meeting you, Ray.

R4 You too, John.

R2 Next time you're in town just give me a call.

R4 I will.

R2 Goodnight, Ray.

R4 Goodnight, John.

R1 Well well.

R3   Fancy.

R4   He understands me.

R1   You

R4   Sees how alone I am.

R1   We're all alone.

R3   We are.

R4   So many nights I've spent trying to find order in chaos.

R3   Find the light when there is only dark.

R1   Looked for love where there is only hate.

R2   When I've said to myself –

R4   When you feel dark.

R3   Mean light.

R4   When you say light.

R1   Mean goodness.

R4   When you say good.

R2   Mean love.

R4   When you say love.

R3   Mean what you say.

R4   When you mean nothing.

R1   Say nothing.

R4   Be silent.

R2   Be still.

R1   Hear your breath.

R3   Enjoy it.

R4   Because it may be your last.

Beat.

R2   I've looked for God through empty glasses
Prayed for light
But there is no remand
No reprieve
From the lies
From the prison.
From the truth that lies in the bottom of my belly
That I know so well.

Beat.

R3   I'm afraid.

R2   Of who I am.

R1   And what I've become.

R3   I feel alone.

R2   Confused.

R1   Depressed.

R4   As I cruise the dark streets the black dog inside me is prowling.

R1   Waiting.

R3   Panting.

R1   In my head.

R4   In my mind.

R2   In my memory.

R3   Blowing the bulbs.

R1   Burning the wires.

R2   Whispering to me.

R4   Get yourself out of this one, fucker.

Beat.

R2   I think of Officer Dibble,
And Top Cat, Benny and the boys.

That city's got dog-catchers.
Picking up the strays.
And taking them to pounds.
In cartoon vans.
With cartoon writing.

R4   But this dog's no cartoon.

R1   And neither is this city.

R4   He's just waiting for the dark.

R1   Biding his time.

R2   As Babylon falls all around me.

Sound of city dub.

R4   Stoned.
         Mashed.
         Wasted.
         Faces pass me by.

R1   Sick.
         Abandoned.
         High.
         Low.

R2   Kissing.
         Shagging.
         Feeling.
         Forgetting.

R4   Like it's the last night on earth.

R2   WHO YOU LOOKING AT?

R1   FUCK OFF.

R3   SLAG.

R2   CUNT.

R1   SLUT.

R3   PRICK.

R2   ARSE-FUCK.

R1   FUCK OFF.

R3   I want to be somebody.

R4   A celebrity.

R1   Not too fat.

R3   Not too thin.

R2   I hate myself.

R4   I love myself.

R1   I wish I was dead.

R4   Haven't you heard the news?

R2   What news?

R4   The end of the world.

R1   My world?

R3   The world.

R2   Fuck the world.

R1   Says who?

R4   The poet.

R2   The Christian.

R1   The drunk.

R3   The whore.

R2   Fuck the poet.

R4   Fuck the Christian.

R3   Fuck the drunk.

R1   Fuck the whore.

R2   Kill the cunts.

R4   Kill them.

R1   A fist smacks a face.

R2   A head hits the wall.

R4   Head spinning.

R1   Bone crunching.

R3   Stars.

R4   Teeth grind.

R2   Boots and fists and bats and bricks.

R4   Explosion.

R1   Dynamite.

R3   Violence.

R2   Anger.

R1   Cordite in the air.

R4   Cold steel of coke.

R2   Clear.

R3   Fast.

R4   Ruthless.

R2   Stiletto.

R4   Stanley knife slashes.

R1   Dark blood from arteries.

R3   From head.

R2   Mouth.

R1   Heart.

R4   Liver.

R3   Kidney.

R2   Brains.

R4   Kill him, kill her.

R2   Kill the cunts, kill them.

R1   Kill the poet.

R4   Kill the drunk.

R2   Kill the Christian.

R3   Kill the whore.

R4   Fuck them.

R2   Rape them.

R1   Split them.

R3   Quarter them.

R1   HANG THEM UP BY THE BALLS TO DRY.

Beat.

R4   The demons slaughter the angels while they sleep
They rampage through damaged minds
Cavort
Orgy
Party.
They whisper in passing ears.

R2   Do it, crazy fucker.

R4   Do it.

R2   Do it.

R4   DO IT!

R1 *pulls a gun. The dub and music cuts.*

R1   Which one?

R4   You want to be a celebrity?

R1   I do.

R2   Front-page news?

R1   That's me.

R4   Then don't shoot the poet.

R1   Why not?

R2   Poetry's dead, nobody'll notice.

R1   The whore, then.

R3   No point, she hates herself already.

R1   The drunk, then?

R4   Too pissed to even notice.

R1   Then the Christian it's got to be.

R2   Do you go to church?

R1   No.

R4   Does anyone you know?

R1   No.

R3   Is it front page news?

R1   I . . .

R4   Is it?

R1   Why the fucking hell does it have to be so
COMPLICATED?

R4   Because the glue that's kept us all together can't hold.

R3   No.

R2   Can't sustain.

R3   No.

R4   The whole thing is turning in on itself.

R3   Mother nature has become UNNATURAL.

R2   Unnatural.

R4   Has gone crazy.

R2   Will soon die of a broken heart.

R1   Fuck.
Mother Nature gone mad?

R3   Yes.

R1   Even now is screaming at the moon?

R2   Yes.

R1   In space?

R4   Yes.

R1   Infinite space?

R2   Yes yes yes.

R1   Will the earth blow up?

R3   Eventually.

R1   Explode?

R2   Possibly.

R1   In slow motion?

R4   Why not?

R1   Like a film?

R2   Yes.

R1   Like poetry?

R3   Yes.

R1   Like painting?

R2   Yes yes yes.

R1   Like a fucking NIGHTMARE!

R4   Yes.

R1   Jesus!

R4   So shoot me.

R3   What?

R2   You heard.

R1   I can't.

R2   Why not?

R1   I think I still love you.

R4   Even though I can't live in my own skin?

R1   I know you've been feeling a bit depressed recently, but I didn't know you felt that bad and anyway you should have said.

R2   You never asked.

R1   How could I?

R4   Didn't you smell a rat when I retreated to my room with a bottle of anti-depressants, a crate of wine and a whole continent of the Colombian?

R1   You said you wanted to be alone.

R2   I did, but when you heard me rant and rave with a bleeding nose and early Leonard Cohen playing continuously on the turntable didn't you ever think of knocking?

R1   I can't say I did, I've known for some time of your unhealthy obsession for vinyl and the past, a lethal combination in anyone's books, wouldn't you say?

R4   Exactly, all the more reason to shoot me.

R1   I can't.

R2   I've let the brittle conscience of charlie rule my brains.

R3   Yes.

R4   The still voice of insanity gain entry to my soul.

R3   Yes.

R2   The wisdom of fools dictate what I think.

R3   Yes.

R4   I've been possessed.

R3   Yes.

R2   Violated.

R3 Yes.

R4 Raped.

R3 Yes.

R2 Abused.

R3 Yes.

R4 Dehumanised by my own self.

R3 Yes.

R2 Now you have the chance to end it.

R4 Stop the rot.

R2 The ugliness.

R3 The lies.

R2 The disease.

R3 The cancer.

R4 Kill me and put an end to it.

R3 Send me to Hell.

R2 For killing love.

R4 Killing myself.

R3 Killing good.

R4 Be my assassin –

R2 Who stands behind me –

R4 With a loaded gun –

R2 Ready to smash muscle, sinew and artery.

R4 Quickly.

R2 Finally.

R3 At rest.

R2 Then left unburied.

R4   Unmourned for.

R3   Unloved.

R4   Burnt.

R2   With my angels.

R4   My demons.

R3   My naked succubae.

R4   Crazed.

R2   Alone.

R3   Forever.

R2   In eternity.

R4   As Babylon falls.
Down below.
On earth.

Beat.

R2   Well?

R3   Well?

R4   Well?

Silence.

R1   Okay.

She shoots. Blood spurts from **R3***'s mouth.* **R2** *falls backwards, apparently dead.* **R1** *keeps the gun pointed.*

Silence.

R4   It's a crazy world.

R1   It is.

R4   Full of crazy people.

R1   Yes.

R4   Like me.

R1   And me.

She drops her arm. **R2** *sits up.* **R4** *wipes the blood from* **R3**'s *face.*
They all stare out.

R4   I'd send her flowers.

R3   I'd wait for them to die.
Then I'd send them back, brown.
I knew you were following me.
I knew it was you that dissolved into the shadows when
I turned my head.
I knew it was your voice I heard at the other end of the line.
You said nothing.
But I knew it was you.
I knew it was.
I knew.

Beat.

R2   It wasn't me.

R3   Then who was it?

R4   It was me.

Beat.

There was a time when all I could see in front of me was
good.

R2   I'd open the window on an early spring day and let in
the sun.

R4   I'd wear a clean cotton shirt.

R2   I'd make some coffee and clean up the remains of the
night.

R4   The smiles.

R1   The laughter.

R2   The half-baked plans and stories still echoing in the
room.

R4   I'd look in the mirror.

R2   I'd recognise the face looking back at me.

R1   It was my face.

R4   If the rooks and ravens were circling then I never heard them.
I was deaf to them and blind to the dark they know lay inside me.

Beat.

I was happy.
There was light in those eyes.
There was love.

R1   Love.

R2   Love.

R3   Love.

R4   You'd be asleep.
One small foot on top of the other.
White pyjamas.
Thin cotton.

R2   Warm.

R3   Snug.

R1   Sweet memory.

R2   You'd wake and say –

R1   What time is it?

R2   Early.

R1   It's still dark.

R2   I know.

R1   What you doing?

R2   Looking up at the stars.

R4   And a blood-red moon.

R3   It's beautiful.

R4   Can you see?

R3   I see.

R1   Come back to bed and make love to me.

R2   I put my arms around her warm body.
She pulls my hand up to her breast.

R1   I love you.

R4   I love you too.

R1   Husband.

R2   Wife.

R3   Lover.

R4   Forever.

R3   Together.

R2   We drive to the mountains.

R1   Then the beach.

R2   We walk into the sea.

R3   We look up at the stars.

R4   We eat fish and chips.

R3   In a polystyrene tray.

R2   With plenty of salt.

R1   And vinegar.

R4   And sauce.

R3   Lovely.

R2   We make love on the beach.

R1   And fuck in the sea.

R4   Like Burt Lancaster. In *From Here to Eternity*.

R3   Then we lie down in the long grass of summer.

R4   On the hills of Llwynbedw.

R1   Looking down into the valley.

R2   I love you.

R1   I love you.

R3   I want us always to be together.

R4   We will.

R2   Forever?

R3   Forever.

R1   Nothing will tear us apart.   (*Beat.*) Come inside me.

R3   Fuck me.

R1   Eat me.

R3   Swallow me.

R1   Make me a mother.

R2   A father.

R4   A saint.

R3   An angel.

R1   A baby.

R2   A son.

R1   A daughter.

R3   A grandmother.

R4   Grandfather.

R2   A lover.
Forever.
Together.

Beat.

R4   But it wasn't to be.
Now I'm afraid that the best years of my life are behind me.
That things will never be like that again.

Will I see her face again?
Will I?
Will I one day wash away the smell of her?
And of what I've done?
What have I done?
What the fuck have I done?

Beat.

R1   Did you think you could just run away?
Change your name?
Become someone else?
Did you?
Did you?

R3   You made your bed, you lie in it.

R4   I never meant to hurt anyone.

R1   But you didn't think.

R2   No.

R3   Couldn't help yourself.

R2   No.

R1   Thought you could just brush it under the carpet and just walk away.

R2   I FUCKING LOVED HER, YOU HEAR!

Beat.

R1   Loved her enough to kill her?

R4   I didn't kill her.

R3   You killed her inside.

R2   She killed me inside.

R1   Only after you killed her first.

R4   No.

R1   Yes, Ray, yes.

R2   Will you quit calling me Ray? I'm not Ray, I never was Ray and I'm not Ray now.

R3   So who are you, Ray?

Beat.

Ray?

R4   I'm just the son of my father.

R3   Who's your father?

R1   His name is Tommy.

R4   He's big mates with Eddie.

R2   Eddie's a butcher. He has a small slaughterhouse opposite his butcher's shop and backing up to the slaughter-house is EC's tyre service.

R1   EC's real name is Edgar but everyone calls him EC.

R4   They amputated his legs just above the knee.

R3   I remember.

R1   EC is superstitious.

R4   He only ever goes on holiday with a fire-extinguisher, a rope, and a hammer.

R3   Tommy buys meat with Eddie. The meat is good. But it isn't cheap. He likes Eddie. Him and Eddie go back a long way.

R2   Both miners once.

R4   Underground and sunshine.

R2   Milk dust sandwiches and the crack
Youngsters nailing other youngsters' wellies to the floor
Long nails
Memories
Wellies like daps
Jesus's daps.

R4   When they shut the mine they shut down a bit of my father too.

R3   I can see him now.

R1   Me too.

R3   Drinking whisky in a chipped cup.

R1   Sitting at the kitchen table he's had since he moved in.

R4   A flat in Chinatown. Council. Rented from Marvin who's shacked up with Beverley.

R1   And your mother?

R3   They had a big bust-up and split up.

R4   Shame.

R3   I must have been about seven. She came home early from work and found me on my own playing outside on a swing.

Sound of swing.

R1   Where's Patsy sweetheart?

R3   In the house.

R1   What's she doing in the house? She's supposed to be baby-sitting you? Sweetheart?

R3   I said nothing.

R1   What I wanted to say is that Daddy came home.

R3   But I can't.
Because I know it'll upset her.
So I purse my lips and carry on swinging.

Sound of swing.

R1   You stay there. I won't be long.

Swing.

R4   She climbs the steps to the second floor.

Swing.

R1   She walks along the corridor till she reaches Number 24.

Swing.

R3   She puts the key in the door.

Swing sound stops.

R4   She goes inside. There's music coming from somewhere, a tune she doesn't recognise.

R1   There's beer tins on the floor. And some quiz show on the TV. She wants to call out but something inside her tells her not to.

R3   She walks down the corridor towards the bedroom. She doesn't know why, but it reminds her of a film she once saw where this French woman stays in her flat and never goes out.

R2   *Repulsion.*

R4   Was it?

R2   Catherine Deneuve was in it.

R3   A blonde woman?

R2   Yeah.

R4   Beautiful.

R2   That's the one.

R3   She reached the bedroom door. It's slightly ajar. She looks through the crack and sees my father on the bed.

R2   With Patsy . . .
The babysitter . . . Fucking.

R1   Like porn stars.

R3   Killing her inside.

R1   She feels numb. She wants to shout out. But nothing comes out. She walks back to the kitchen. She sits down. She sees a bloke on the quiz show looking tense.
She wonders what question's been asked to make him look like that.

R4   She goes and stands in the mirror.
Looking at her face.
Does she know the woman looking back at her?
She used to be beautiful.

R1   They said she'd go places that the sun would shine in her soul, it's what they said. People would stop and stare in the street. There was light in her, a dancing light. And a fire glowing within. She could have had the whole world at her feet.

R2   Was a time when she didn't need anyone to tell her she just . . . Am I still beautiful? Am I?

R3   She smashes the mirror. The fucking sounds from the bedroom stop. She picks a knife up from the table, turns around and he's standing there looking at her and then she comes out too . . . Patsy.
She notices she's got clotted cream on her breasts.
He did that once with me and he licked it all off.
He said he loved me . . . then.
He said he'd never leave me.
He said I was the love of his life.

R1 *runs at* **R2** *with a knife, they wrestle. He hits her. The knife falls.*

R4   FUCKING BITCH!

R3   You all right?

R2   I had no fucking choice.

R3   You all right?

R4   She was going to kill me.

R3   You all right?

R2   Fucking cunt.

R3   You all right?

R4   Fucking whore.

R3   You all right?

R2   I never loved her.

R3   You all right?

R4   Didn't even fancy her.

R3   You all right?

R2   It was her who wanted it.

R3   You all right?

R2   Fuckin' nick-nacks.

R3   You all right?

R2   All over the fucking house.

R3   You all right?

R2   Fuckin' trinkets.

R3   You all right?

R4   Fuckin' nutcase.

R3   You all right?

R2   Fuckin' . . .

R4   Fuckin' . . .

R1   I'm all right.

R4   She's all right.

R1   I'm not all right.

R2   She's not all right.

R4   She is.

R1   I am.

R2   SEE!
She's a whore.

R1   What?

R4   Whore.

R3 I should go.

R2 Whore.

R3 I'll text you.

R4 No.

R3 I'll call you then.

R2 No.

Beat.

R3 What then?

R4 I'm coming with you.

R3 You leaving her?

R2 Yeah.

R3 Now?

R4 Don't you love me?

R3 What?

R2 You said.

R3 I only –

R4 YOU'RE JUST LIKE FUCKING HER!

Beat.

R1 You all right?

R2 Her.

R1 You all right?

R4 You're a whore.

R1 You all right?

R2 I don't love you.

R1 You all right?

R4 CUNT.

R1 You all right?

R2 TWO CUNTS.

R1 You all right?

R4 I'm not a CUNT. YOU HEAR ME? I . . . AM . . . NOT . . . A . . . CUNT.

Beat.

YOU TWO . . . YOU AND YOU . . . ARE –

Beat.

CUNTS.

Long silence.

R2 This morning. This very morning. This morning right . . . I . . . was going to put it all behind me. I fuckin' . . . all of it . . . be . . . hind . . . me.

R4 My point is. My first point is . . . is . . . WILL YOU JUST LET ME FINISH, CUNTS?

Silence.

R2 (*to head*) Everything is in here. Nothing else is worth a jacksy. Born alone, die alone. (*Beat.*) I'm ill. I am fucking ill. But I can't pick up the phone. I've never been able to pick up the phone.

R3 I think I should go.

Beat.

I'm going.

Beat.

It's for the best.

Beat.

I'm sorry.

Beat.

I just wanted . . . I . . . (*Beat.*) I'll post the keys through the letterbox.

Silence.

We hear the sound of dubbed footsteps. Then a door slams. The keys land on the floor.

R1   It's over.

R4   Yes.

R1   Finished.

R4   Yes.

R1   Forever.

R4   Yes. I've been a cunt to you.

R2   I didn't love you.
I liked the way you smelt, that's all.
You used to try so hard.
It broke my heart.
I didn't love you.

R1   I wanted another child with you.
I told my mother we were going to have a child.
She clapped her hands.

R4   I didn't belong. I've never belonged. Anywhere.

R1   We got lost in the storm.

R2   Yeah.

R1   You couldn't move on.

R4   No.

R1   You're rotting from inside out.

R2   I am. If it wasn't for those pigeons I'd already be dead . . .

Beat.

R1   I don't think you loved anyone, Tommy.

R4   Maybe you're right . . . but what's love?

R1   That may haunt you forever.

R2   Who knows.

R4   Undress.

Beat.

R1   What?

R4   Let me fuck you one last time and breathe no more.
I want you to swallow me
Suck me
Be sucked
Digested
Had
Consumed
Eaten
Burnt
See stars
Knowing it'll be the last time I'll ever see your cunt again.

Beat.

R1   No.

R2   Please.

R1   No.

R2   I'M FUCKING BEGGING YOU!

R1   It's over, Tommy.

Beat.

You put the jewels of my soul in bin-liners and left them for
the rubbish men.
I can't forgive you for that.
I'm walking away, Tommy.
And I'm never coming back.

R4   Don't go, Mammy . . . don't go . . . MAMMY!

R2   You belong with her, not me. Go. Got to your mother.
I SAID GO TO YOUR MOTHER.

R4   That's the last time I saw him.
He moved into the flat in Chinatown.

R3   Rented it. From Marvin. Who's shacked up with
Beverley.

R4   The flat's empty, Tommy.

R3   Says Marv.

R4   You can have it till I need it back, I'm moving to
Cwmphil with Beverley.

R2   You sure?

R4   I'm sure.

R1   Tommy looks at Marv in the eye. His good eye. His
bad eye looked the wrong way, leaving Clancy's after an all-
night party in Ma Clancy's old Volvo. He was alone, save
for a party can and twenty Regal. Black ice. Good eye turns
bad looking in the wrong direction. Six weeks in a coma.
Never the same. Good with cars, but always something, a
nut here or a bolt there he forgets to put back.

R3   Would you rent a flat from a man who takes out a
gear box on a 1963 Volkswagen Campervan with split
windscreen only to put a new secondhand one back in with
four reverse gears and blame the diff?

R4   It was the diff!

R2   Diff be buggered.

R4   It fuckin' was, on British cars, right. The diff can only
go in one way but with some foreign cars the diff can go in
either way, anyone could tell you that.

R2   Foreign cars, yeah, like the fuckin' Volvo or Fiat, yeah,
but not the fuckin' VOLKSWAGEN, Marvin.

R4   I'm not listening to this.

R2   Marvin?

R4   Aching, you are. Aching to fall out with someone.
Well, you're not fucking falling out with me. I'm not getting
involved. I am staying well out of it.

R2   Where you going?

R4   To buy a canoe.

R2   A what?

R4   You heard, to go out on the river.

R2   A canoe.

R3   I'm done with cars, cars fuck your head up. If anybody
asks me about cars again I'm going to turn round and say get
a canoe. FUCK CARS THE FUTURE IS IN CANOES.

R2   Marv, come back, Marv! Marv!

R3   But he didn't come back. Dad took the flat and Marv
moved to Cwmphil.

R1   Happy days.

R4   But Dad's got a rat in his skull.
A pain in his side.
A black dog inside him.
But he won't pick up the phone.
If only he'd pick up the phone.

R1   You're just a bit depressed, that's all, you haven't been
the same since those pigeons got lost in Antwerp.

R3   Says Emrys the slaughterman one day in the
slaughterhouse.

R2   Ronnie Llwynbedw's pigeons come back in record
time.

R1   But Dad's never did.

R4   He loved them pigeons.

R3   He loved them more than me and my mother.

R4 Give me a hand, says Emrys.

R2 In the steam and the flesh and the fleeces.

R4 Tommy watches Emrys load up the gun, shoots one, two, three with the humane killer, then slits one, two, three necks.

R1 Heavy bastards see, Tommy.

R2 Yeah.

R1 Drizzled coats, standing out in the rain all night. I reckon they do it on purpose, they know they're going to die so they say fuck it, if I'm getting skinned from my arse to my neck then I'm going to make it difficult for the bastards. So they stand out in the rain chewing grass. All night making their woolly coats heavy. Whoever said sheep were thick? You want to have a go?

R2 No, I'm all right.

R1 Sure?

R2 Yeah. Killing's not really my dap, Em.

R1 Don't say I never offered.

R2 No . . . I won't. Eddie over the shop, is he?

R1 Should be.

R3 It's a quarter to six when Dad walks into Eddie's shop.

R2 It's now or never.

R3 He hears Eddie talk out back on the phone. Eddie shouts on the phone like nobody Tommy knows.

R4 Fucking hell, Tom, I thought you'd emigrated.

R2 No.

R4 How you been?

R2 OK.

R4 What can I get you?

R2   Few lamb chops, Ed.

R4   Four?

R2   Make it two.

R4   Two forty-eight, Tommy, how's that?

R2   Lovely.

R4   Fifty-two pence and two quid, how's that?

R2   Eddie.

R4   Yeah?

R2   Don't think I'm being funny, but I was wondering if you could do me a favour.

R4   No problem, Tom, what can I do for you?

R2   I'd like to keep it between you and me, you got me?

R4   Got you, nobody need know, Tom, nobody, what you got on your mind?

R2   I want . . . you to take me down the stores . . .

R4   The stores.

R2   Yeah.

Beat.

And weigh me.

R4   Weigh you?

R2   Yeah. Will you do it?

R4   What the fuck for?

R1   Tommy looks at Eddie.

R3   Eddie looks back at Tommy.

R1   And suddenly the penny drops.

R3   Eddie knows.

R4   Thirteen-seven.

R2   You sure?

R4   Positive.
You been to the doctor, Tom?

R2   Fuck doctors.

R4   Might do you good.

R2   I can't pick up the phone.
I've never been able to pick up the phone.

Beat.

Same time next week?

R4   Yeah.

R2   Nobody else knows, got it?

R4   Nobody.

R2   Thanks.

R4   Look after yourself, Tom.

R2   I will.

R1   Tommy leaves. Eddie watches him go: Mrs Eddie joins him.
She pulls down the blinds.

R4   What we having for tea?

R1   Faggots.

R3   Tommy watches soap with a can of cheap lager.

R1   He hates soap.

R3   He switches off the TV.

R1   The only sound is him swallowing lager. Cold. Last one in the fridge. He feels it down in his stomach.

R3   He crushes the tin.

R1   Tommy eats.

R3   Lamb chops.

R1   He eats the fat.

R3   All of it.

R1   He's thinking of chewing the bones.

R3   Then thinks again and chucks them in the bin.

R1   He can't sleep.

R3   He's got a pain in his side.

R2   Raging.

R3   He lights a fag standing up at the window looking down over Chinatown.

R1   An hour passes.

R3   He's got no more fags.

R1   He crushes the packet.

R3   Dr Harris's phone number stares him right in the face.

R1   But he can't pick up the phone.

R3   He's never been able to pick up the phone.

R1   If he did I'd have told him that despite everything that's happened –

R3   I loved him.

R4   Happy birthday, Dad.

R2   Thanks.

R4   Did you get my card?

R2   Yes.

R4   James Dean.

R2   Yeah.

R4   Dream like you live forever. Live like you die today.

R2   Yeah.

R4   Sorry I couldn't be there today.

R2 That's all right.

R4 I'm working.

R2 Yeah.

R4 You OK?

R2 I'm fine.

R4 Got any plans?

R2 It's quiz night in The Crown.

R4 That's good.
I love you, Dad.

Beat.

Dad?

Beat.

R2 I love you too.

R4 Good. (*Beat.*) Take care.

R2 And you.

Beat.

R3 But he never did.

R1 One, two, three months go by. Every Friday on the
scales at Eddie's.

R3 Thirteen-four.

R1 Thirteen-one.

R3 Twelve-ten.

R1 Twelve-six.

R3 And receding.

R4 Thirteen-four, honest to God.

R3 Tommy looks at Eddie. Takes out his notebook.
Eddie watches.

R4   Honest.

R1   Tommy looks him in the eye.
Writes less in his book. Less. In capital letters.

R4   He's dying.

R3   Who is?

R4   Tommy is.

R1   Says Eddie to Mrs Eddie that night.

R3   How do you know?

R4   I seen him change.

R3   What's changed?

R4   I see him out walking night and day. I look but he
don't look up.

R3   So?

R4   Tommy's a proud man. You never catch him not
looking up.

R1   Eddie stands in the bedroom mirror with only his pants
and pyjama top. Mrs E has gone to the bathroom.
His legs are getting skinny, but shit, thinks E to himself.

R4   I'm still here, I'm still fucking here.

R3   Tommy lies in newly cut grass
In the field he remembers working in during the summers
No bailing then, just a rake to turn over the hay
And cider.

R1   And Cyril hiding moles under his hat.

R3   Cyril was an ex-soldier. Gone crazy.

R1   Some said he was moonstruck but nobody knows.

R3   Tommy looks around the empty field and down
towards the river. He remembers it as the place that
Leighton Owen drowned all those years ago. On the

riverbank he sees an eel stuck on a forgotten night-line. It's belly up. He walks into the river in his shoes.

R1   He enjoys the sensation of water on his feet, then his knees.

R4   Tommy!

R1   Tommy spins round and sees Eddie, looking down at him from the bridge.

R3   Tommy looks at Eddie and Eddie at Tommy.
Eddie knows.

R1   And so does Tommy.

R3   It's a quarter to six. Eddie's brushing out the shop. It's Friday. He looks up at Chinatown. No sign of Tommy.
Mrs E pulls down the blinds.

R4   He hasn't been.

R1   Perhaps he'll come tomorrow.

R3   Mrs E gets on the scales. Eddie weighs her.

R4   Nine stone eleven.

R1   That's good.

R4   It is.

R3   And Eddie means it. As he watches his wife walk away. He's glad that to her he doesn't lie.

R1   Eddie knocks on Tommy's door. But there's no reply.

R4   Because Tommy's not there.

R1   And he'll never be there again.

R4   Tommy's on a train. Looking at his reflection in the glass.
As the world passes him by.
He thinks he looks like his father by now.

R3   Or is it his father before that?
There's no turning back time.

R4   And cancer's a cunt.

R2   I've been a cunt
But I'm a cunt no more
Forgive me
I'm sorry
I never meant to hurt anyone
If I knew what love was I'd have loved you
But I was blind
I couldn't see
But now I can.
I don't think there's ever been a time when I can see more clearly.

R1   He looks at the sky
And the earth all around.

R2   It won't be long now, it won't be long.

R4   Pigeons fly, he had told me once, fathers travel by train.

Beat.

R3   He got into Antwerp at six.

R1   To be with his pigeons.
He checked into a hotel.
On Santa Ana Strasse.
Room 24.

R4   It was nothing special.
It was just a room.

R1   Anonymous.

R4   Corporate.

R2   Functional.

R3   With a double bed.

R1   Desk and chair.

R2   En-suite bathroom.

R4   And in the drawer a Bible.
And underneath the Bible a handwritten note.

'One may have a blazing hearth in one's soul yet no one
ever comes to sit by it. Passers-by see only a wisp of smoke
rising from the chimney and continue on their way.'

R2   Sainte Beuve. Spelt S-A-I-N-T-E. The E's a dead
giveaway. Obviously French.

R1   But is it a he or a she?

R2   Hard to tell.

R3   Did Sainte Beuve write it down or was somebody just
quoting something he or she had written before?

R1   Why go to the trouble? Isn't it just a fancy way of
saying no one gives a fuck? Born alone.

R2   Die alone.

R1   Get on with it.

R2   No big deal.

R4   Dad wrote the note.

R3   Ah.

R4   It was the last thing he did.

R2   The black dog inside me is prowling
Waiting
Panting
In my head
In my mind
Blowing the bulbs
Fusing the fuses
Whispering in my ear
It's only a matter of time, fucker.

R4   He looks out of the windo
At the sleeping city
And the endless sky
He knows they're out there somewhere and one day he'll
find them.

Beat.

So he kills the black dog
And in so doing he kills himself.
He dies in his sleep, peacefully
And floats up to the sky
He has a smile on his face
He is happy.

R2   Man and pigeon united.

R4   Son bereaved.
If only he'd picked up the phone I could have said
I love you, Dad.

R1   I love you.

R3   I love you.

R4   I am the son of my father.

Silence.

R1   Love.

R2   Love.

R3   Love.

Beat.

R4   Is love the only drug left in this world that can make
life bearable? Is it? Is it?

R1   I'd like to think so.

R2   What happens if you think you're in love but you find
out later that you're not?

R3   That you thought you did but you didn't?

R2   Yes.

R3   That you've never really felt it?

R2   Yes.

R1   Never really known it?

R2 Yes.

R4 What kind of person does that make you?

R2 Have you thought about it?

R1 I have.

R3 Me too.

R4 I've thought about it plenty.
I've walked the night thinking about it.
Taken train rides to towns I'd never been to and thought about it.
Stayed in no-star hotels where I was the only guest and thought about it.
Taken breakfast there alone and thought about it.

R2 One sausage.

R1 One egg.

R3 Strip of bacon.

R4 Tinned tomato.

R1 Instant coffee.

R3 White toast.

R4 HP Sauce.

R2 Distant radio in the background.
Playing local radio.

R1 Adverts for fast-food places.

R4 Hairdressers.

R3 Plumbers.

R1 DIY stores.

R4 Computer stores.

R1 I've thought about it more often than I like to remember.

R2 I've woken in a cold sweat thinking about it.

R1   With a guilt you can cut with a knife.

R3   Guilt's a killer.

R4   I'd stand looking out of the window.

R2   Staring at nothing.

R4   She'd wake and say –

R3   What time is it?

R4   Early.

R3   It's still dark.

R2   I know.

R3   I'm trying to sleep.

R4   I'm sorry.

R3   Can't you go downstairs?

R4   I go downstairs
Turn on the radio
Chew toast
Making notes in my head
Walk around the kitchen
Bare boards
Floorboards
Fat anxiety
In my belly
In my head
In my mind.

R2   Does she know that I'm slowly going insane?

R4   I pop a pill.

R2   To settle.

R4   Drink Vit C.

R2   Monday morning.

R4   My limbs are heavy.

R2 I look in the mirror.

R4 The whites of my eyes are on holiday in off-yellow.
And have been for some time.

R2 Should drink more water
But I can't stand the stuff
Never have
I piss
Feel heavy
No energy
Do they know what's inside my head?
Do they?

R4 Does that obnoxious cunt with the bad eye-contact
know?

R2 Does he know that I know?

R4 Does he know how much I hate him?

R2 I want to tell him.
I want to say –

R4 Do you know how often I've come inside her? On her?
With her? Do you know how my cock twitches when I think
of her? Do you?

R2 Do I? I do.

R4 His wife. Why doesn't he say something?
Why doesn't he follow me to the gents one day.
Slam me up against the wall and say –

R2 You fuck her again and I'll kill you.

R4 His manicured, well-kept thumb and forefinger are on
my jaw.
My cheeks bear his fingerprints.

R2 You understand, fucker? Do you?

R4 But I'm not afraid
I want him to hurt me
So that I can feel

Not feel numb
Because this is how I am
Numb.
How I became like this I don't know
It didn't just happen
It crept up on me
Without me knowing
Maybe if he hit me it would go away
If he drew blood
If my lip split
If the bone in my nose
Smashed
And my eyes watered
Maybe the film would lift
I'd see clearly
Feel again
Taste blood in my mouth
Know the feeling of crushed bone
Real
Connected
I'd thank him for killing the numb in me.
'You've killed the numb in me, now I can see.'
He might spit the word cunt at me
Then release me
Walk away
I'd hear his footsteps disappear
The inner door shut
The outer door slam
I could slide down the wall
With a real smile on my face
I could sit there with my arse on my ankles
Bleeding.
I'd hear the water jets of the urinal spring to life
I might laugh
Enjoying the echo
My own voice
My reclaimed real self
Laughing
Bleeding

Connected
Me.

R2   Me.

R1   Me.

R3   Me.

R2   But he won't.

R4   Not the type.

R2   He'd do anything but give me life.

R4   Cunt.

R3   Give me real.

R4   Fucker.

R2   Kill the numb.

R1   Selfish prick.

R2   I hate him. Almost as much as I hate myself.

R4   Who am I?

R1   A businessman too?

R2   A selfish fucker.

R3   A lover.

R1   A poet.

R3   A Christian.

R2   A whore.

R4   I swallow
A mouthful
I spit it out
I feel sick
I can't go on like this
I can't eat
Can't fuck
Can't love

No one to love.
I reach for the bottle
Unscrew the cap
Swig
Feels warm in my belly
In the back of my throat
Swig again
Put it back
Think
Fuck it
I put it in my bag
Fuck it.

R2   Fuck it.

R1   Fuck it.

R3   Fuck it.

R4   I can't go on any more. I can't.
I just . . .
Who would have ever thought that it would come to this?

R3   Not me.

R1   Or me.

R4   I can't bear to think of him fucking her.

R2   I hate him.

R4   I can see him now. In a hotel room. Somewhere in
Europe.
Pressing his trousers.
In a trouser-press.
Like some big-shot businessman.
Who does he think he is?

R1   Is he a businessman?
Does he press his trousers?
In a hotel room?
In a city?
Not his.
Can you describe it?

R2   If somebody asked me I'd say it's nothing special.
It's just a room.

R4   I thought it was just me and him.

R3   The husband and the lover.

R4   We both stayed in the same hotel in the same room
on separate occasions and the common denominator was
my wife.

R1   Was?

R4   What if I said that we've both also stayed in this room
on several occasions but not at the same time.

R2   That we both checked in alone.
But didn't necessarily spend the night alone.

R4   So with whom did we spend it?
Did my wife know?
Did his?
Has he got a wife?

R3   Whose story is this?

R2   Whose identity are we protecting here?

R3   Mine.

R2   Or his?

R4   Who is he?

R2   Where am I?

R3   How did we get here?

R1   Which one of us in this room is so lost
So disconnected from their own self that all they are is a bag
of bones with thoughts? A husk.
Walking round their own life like a stranger.
Incoherent.
Not even sure of what is made up or memory.

R2   Just bums.

R4   Bums at the edge of someone else's story.

R1   Whose story?

R2   What are the possibilities?

R4   What is the scenario here?
What is it that we suppose happened?

R2   Fake or coincidence?

R1   Truth or lie?

R2   What the fuck's happened?
TELL ME WHAT THE FUCK'S HAPPENED!

R1   Let's go back to the room.

R2   The hotel room?

R1   Yes. Describe it.

R4   It's nothing special.

R2   It's just a room.

R3   Comfortable but anonymous.

R2   Corporate.

R4   Functional.

R3   Standard.

R4   Double bed.

R2   Desk and chair.

R3   Built-in wardrobe with iron and ironing board.

R2   Small safe.

R4   Spare pillows.

R3   Tea and coffee and Highland biscuits . . .

R4   And I'm alone.

R2   Waiting for a stranger.

R3   A perfect stranger.

R2   To knock on my door.

Beat.

R4   Come in. Sit down. Make yourself at home.

R2   Do you want to sit here?

R4   Sit here.

R2   No no, sit here.

R4   Do you mind if I call you John?

R2   People don't understand, see, John.
Don't know what I've gone through.

R4   Let's just say big business fucked up my life.
Or to be precise a businessman did, a businessCUNT.

R2   I was content.

R4   Had no idea anything was wrong.

R2   I trusted her.

R4   I thought she trusted me.

R1   Trust means a lot to me. It's important to me.

R3   It's in the top three qualities I look for in a person.

R1   Trust.

R3   Love.

R1   Loyalty.

R3   Big three.

R1   Big time.

R3   Always.

R4   But not easy to find.

R1   No.

R2   Not in my experience, anyway.

R3   No.

R4   Not in one person.

R2   Take what happened tonight.

R4   I've cracked open a red.

R2   Put two glasses out ready.

R4   When right out of the blue she calls.

R2   Hello.

R1   It's Caroline.

R4   Oh hi.

R1   I'm running late.

R3   How late?

R1   I don't know, it's hard to say.

R4   Where are you?

R1   There's been an accident.

R2   Are you OK?

R1   I'm fine but I'm in a jam, a traffic jam, it's gridlocked.

R3   Are you in a taxi?

R1   Yes.

R2   What's happened?

R1   The taxi driver's heard that a double-decker has collided or tried to avoid a woman with a pram.

R2   Does he know what she looks like?

R1   I don't think so, it happened up ahead, I'll be there as soon as possible.

R3   OK. Keep in radio contact.

R1   I will.

R2   And be careful.

R4   Then the phone went dead.

R2   Now there's a few things I want you to consider about that conversation.

R4   One.

R2   Take Caroline.

R4   You'll notice I said, are you OK? Then later on I also said, and be careful.

R2   Now Caroline isn't someone I know that well, in fact I'd never met her until tonight. I've only ever spoken to her on the phone. Tonight was going to be the first time I'd met her in the flesh. Now normally someone you know as fleetingly as I know Caroline would have just said fine, get here when you can, it's no problem, they might even have been angry with her for fucking up your well laid plans, but not me.

R4   I said straightaway, are you OK? Then I followed that up with and be careful. I think she appreciated that.
In fact, I know she appreciated that because when she did eventually show up looking a little flustered she said –

R1   Thanks for your concern, I appreciate it.

R3   No worries. Drink?

R1   Why not?

R4   Vodka?

R1   Lovely.

R2   Large?

R1   Small.

R3   Tonic?

R1   Please.

R2   Lemon?

R1   A slice.

R4   Ice?

R1   Two lumps.

R2   Cheers.

R3   Sit down.

R4   How long can you stay?

R1   How long would you like me to stay?

R4   Couple of hours.

R3   Can we talk first?

R1   We can do whatever you like.

R2   Will you show me your arse?

R1   Can we get the money out of the way first?
I have a friend if you're interested.

R2   Really?

R1   Really.
She does everything.

R3   Oh?

R1   Shall I call her?

R2   Sit down . . . please.

R4   She sat. She was safe. Consideration number one
complete.

R2   Point two is the accident itself. What was the woman
doing out after midnight with a baby in the pram?

R4   Was she homeless?

R2   Destitute?

R4   Had nowhere to go?

R2   Did she absent-mindedly step into the path of a double-
decker bus because she had so much on her mind?

R4   Did she instinctively put her head into the pram to
protect her innocent child?

R2 Is that why the bus driver, ever alert, slams on his breaks and managed to swerve to avoid her, saving the child and the woman, but unfortunately ploughs straight first into a late-night cyber café lit by neon where half-a-dozen insomniacs are surfing the web or chatting to other people with made-up names? Is it?

R4 They never had the chance.
One bloke was in the middle of writing 'I love you' to his girlfriend in Australia, at least that's what the paper said, unless they made it up.
Never stood a chance.
Never saw it coming.
And all the while the mother, like any good mother should, is protecting her child, her strong arms around the bundle of cotton and polyester which is her joy.

R3 My baby, my baby.

R4 She shouts as half-a-dozen people lose their lives.

R2 But there is no baby.

R1 There never was a baby.

R2 All that's inside the pram is the woman's belongings, her worldly goods.

R3 And two cans of Stella.

R1 Wrapped up in cotton.

R4 Her life and joy.

R2 She looks at the horror in front of her.

R3 Chaos.

R1 Carnage.

R4 Will she be able to live with herself for causing all this? Or will the police find her the next morning with a syringe of smack in her retina because she doesn't like what her eyes have seen?

R2   A lot of people wouldn't find it in their hearts to forgive her.
They'd blame her for being pissed and high.

R4   But not me.

R2   I forgave her.

R4   I feel for her.

R2   She's not innocent but she's not guilty. She's just human.

R4   Like you.

R2   And me.

R1   She has to live with herself.

R3   She has to imagine the girlfriend in Australia.

R4   In Queensland.
On a sunny morning.
Smiling at what her boyfriend's just written.

R2   Fuck me to death and Hell.
I love you.

R1   She wonders why he doesn't reply.

R4   She doesn't know that those words are the last words he'll ever write.

R3   I wasn't sure I loved him till that moment.

R2   But she does now.
When she sees what he'd written.

R3   He's got a way with words.
The mind that makes up the words that puts pen to paper or finger to keys I've always liked.

R1   But now she loves.

R2   And that's worse.

R4   And with sun-tanned slender fingers stained with fresh pineapple she replies.

R3   Greetings from the jungle.
Crocydylys.
I love you too.
I'll be home soon.
X.

R2   The imaginary mother has to live with this.
If she survives.
If she goes through rehab.
And the person who loves her will have to be strong.
He'll have to be there in the middle of the night when she
wakes from her nightmares screaming.

R1   Kill me, kill me, kill me, kill me, kill me.

R4   I pity the dead.
And I forgive the living.
We're all fragile.
That's why I'm a sensitive man.
I forgive.
Which brings me to my final point.

R2   In my conversation with Caroline you may remember
that I asked what the mother looked like.
The reason for that is quite simple.

R4   It could have been my wife.

R1   Ex-wife.

R3   She always wanted a baby.
A child.

R2   The fruit of our union.

R1   But we never did.

R4   That night for some strange reason.
I thought it could have been her.
Pushing her baby.

R2   His baby.

R4   In a pram.

R2   Why'd she be pushing a pram at that time of night?

R1   Has she finally realised that he's not the man for her?

R2   Has she finally realised that she still loves me and always has?

R4   Should I forgive her?

R2   Or has he kicked her out?

R1   Sent her out to a hundred-mile desert.

R2   Till the sun cooks her.

R4   Roasts her.

R2   Burns her to a crisp.

R4   Has she been shafted?

R2   By a businessman?

R4   A businesscunt?

R2   Cufflinked.

R4   Trouser-pressed.

R2   Bolloxed.

R4   Like me.

R2   And me?

R4   Can I forgive her?

R2   Should I forgive her?

R4   Can I take her back?

R1   Can we turn back the clock?

R3   We went to The Perseverance.
It's a gastropub not far from here.

R4   From an extensive menu I ordered the devilled kidneys.
Just for the hell of it.

R3   I ordered the frittata.

R4   Nice.

R2 Over the course of the evening she told me things that hitherto I knew nothing about.

R4 The waiter had just opened the second bottle of the Portuguese Segada when she turned to me and said.

R3 I've been a cunt to you. I'm sorry.

R2 Good God.

R3 A few months ago while I was away working I got drunk, I think I blacked out. I woke up with a man in my bed and bruising on my thighs. I think I fucked him.

R4 You think?

R3 I fucked him. I'm sorry.

R2 Was that the only time?

R1 No. The second time was a month later. I ran away into a field near the airport and in that field he fucked me again. I was so full of self-loathing I couldn't come home.

R4 Was that the last time?

R3 The third time was only three weeks ago. I met him in a bar you never go to. We got drunk and I snogged him. I told him it had to stop.

Beat.

I'm so sorry. Really I am.

R2 I feel sick.

R1 I know, but I had to tell you. I couldn't go on not telling you. I'm sorry. I'm really sorry.

R2 I swallow the Segada. I've never known a wine to taste so bitter.

R1 I'm going to have to go to the toilet.

R2 She gets up and I watch her go, annoyed at myself that I'm looking at her arse, angry that I feel a tightness in my groin, my cock hardening.

R4   I feel the eyes of the restaurant upon me even though nobody's heard. Nobody's seen. I feel humiliated. Do I know this man? Is he here in the restaurant watching for my response? Is it a game they're playing? Is is that broad-shouldered cunt with his back to me sitting in the window? It can't be, he'd have missed my reaction, and besides his face is familiar I'm sure I've seen him on TV.
Maybe he doesn't live in this city.

R2   Maybe that's a good thing. If he did, I think I'd have to kill him. Or he'd have to kill me. I am intrigued to know what he looks like. Is he big? Is he small? How reasonable will he be when one of his eyeballs is like jelly in my hand and his balls are in the fruit bowl his wife recently bought in Ikea?

Beat.

R4   I look at the knife on the table. I imagine my hand curling round it, holding it like the handshake of a long-lost friend.

R2   WHAT THE FUCK IS SHE DOING IN THE TOILET?!

R1   It's got to stop.

R4   I can't.

R1   You're married.

R4   So are you.

R1   It's over.

R4   No. Let me fuck you one more time.
Then breathe no more.
Swallow me.
Fuck me.
Digest me.
Don't discard me.
I want to be eaten.
Possessed.
Burnt.

See stars.
Knowing it will be the last time I'll ever see your cunt again.

R1   No.

R4   I beg you.

R2   She comes back from the toilet.
Her eyes are red and puffy.
Do I know him?

R3   No.

R2   You sure?

R1   Yes.

R2   Who is he?

R3   Nobody.

R2   Who is he, BITCH?

R1   He's just a businessman.
A business executive.
For a large multinational.

R2   Cunt.
I pour her some wine.
My mind is on fire.
I keep thinking of his hands on her body, his cock inside her.
He must have been rough if he bruised her.

R3   I'm sorry.

R4   It's my fault.

R1   Don't punish yourself.

R4   How can I not when my insides are burning.
Like a half-empty oil tanker.
Abandoned.
The crew gone.
The captain dead.
And a storm approaching.
I can't live in my own skin.
I can't breathe.

R3 I think you're depressed.

R2 Oh, really?

R1 I'm not coming home.
Don't try to follow me.
Don't try to contact me.
It's over.
If you send me flowers.
I'll wait for them to die.
Then I'll send them back brown.
We're finished.

R4 Time freezes around me.
I think of her and the life we shared.
The life we could still be having now.
I could be kissing her lips.
Stroking her breasts.
Feeling a heaviness in my cock on a spring morning.

R2 The baby growing silently inside her that I know
nothing about.

R3 I'm pregnant.

R2 It's not mine. I know it's not.

R1 Did you hear me?

R2 It's not my baby, the father is a man I've never met
who fucked her in places I've never been.

Beat.

R4 He's already a dead man.

R2 And so am I.
Different reality.
Different life.
Different man.

R4 There must be many like me.
I pity them.
I am dead.

I killed myself at the loins of whores in the lust of the city
night.
And it won't let me go.
I look at the man I used to be.
In black and white, a photograph.
That man is no longer.
Me.

Beat.

R1   Well?

R2   Well what?

R1   Aren't you going to say something?

R2   Frost is surrounding my heart.
An icicle has opened a wound.
Which will slowly bleed me to death.

R1   DON'T JUST LOOK AT ME LIKE THAT.
SAY SOMETHING!

As the next speech develops, **R1**, **R2** *and* **R3** *echo occasional words
and sentences alternately, building to a rhythmic climax.*

R4/R2   I can't speak. I can't move. I am an abandoned
ship on a calm ocean. Searing heat. So hot I can't breathe.
Feel like a chicken in an oven roasting on a spit. There's a
see-through oven door I can see out. I can see her legs.
She's got the radio on and a summer dress. He comes into
the room. I can't see his face. I can see his hand on her
arse. She's smiling back. She pinches his cock and he
watches her cleaning the vegetables. Was a time when I did
that, parsnips, potatoes, swedes, carrots, broccoli, the whole
nine yards. Always thought she loved me, would never leave
me, would stick by me thick and thin and thin and thick.
Now she's fucking someone else in front of me. He's pulling
at her dress, sucking her breasts, he's got his cock out, she's
holding it in her hand, he goes down on her, he's got her
cunt juice all over his face. I'm sick. I smash my head
against the glass oven door. I throw up. She's fucking him.

SHE CAN'T SEE, CAN'T HEAR, I SCREAM OUT HER
NAME OVER AND OVER. THE HEAT AND THE
NOISE IS FUCKING UNBEARABLE, UNBEARABLE.

Etc. to climax.

Silence.

R4   I open my eyes.
She's nowhere to be seen.
I'm alone. And I'm no longer at home. The name on my
passport isn't mine and I have no ring on my finger. Who
I am and where I come from nobody knows. Those who
think they know me call me Ray. I'm crazy Ray. I'm in
Room 24 of the Big Sleep Hotel.

R1   Corporate.

R2   Anonymous.

R3   Functional.

R2   But I have the strange feeling that the room isn't really
here.

R1   Did you imagine it?

R3   Is it a dream?

R2   Where am I?

R4   My fingers are brown with nicotine.

R1   Some night.

R3   Some day.

R4   My lips are stained red.

R1   Lipstick or red wine?

R2   Or a combination of both?

R4   There are fag burns on my shirt.
Stains all over my trousers.
My pants and socks are
Hidden under a leather skirt.

And a black bra.
And high heels.

R2   And some condoms.
Used.

R4   Fuck.
I put my hand inside my shirt.
Feels sticky.
Is is blood?

R2   I take it off.
Something is written on my chest in crayon.
Or is it lipstick?
I can make out an S.
In the mirror it spells T . . . U . . . L . . . S.
From my chest to my belly.

R4   I am a slut.

R3   A whore.

R4   Someone is lying in the bed. I can't see who it is. I lift
the sheet. It's a woman. She doesn't make a noise. Is she
dead?

R2   Who is she?

R4   Is that blood on her?
Is that blood on the sheets?

R1   Have you got blood on your hands?
Do you ruin everything you touch?
Who are you?

R2   Is that my wife?

R4   Is that you?

R1   What the fuck's happened here?
Who wrote 'SLUT' on your chest?
Where have you been?
What the fuck is going on?
Can't you hear me?

R4   Yes.

R1   Can't you see me?

R2   Yes.

R1   Then look at me you CUNT!

R4   I hear the sound of a flush.
The bathroom door opens. A second woman comes out.
She's naked. Beautiful. A body to die for.

R2   Your wife?

R4   Is it?
She looks at me and says –

R3   Hi.

R4   Hi.

R2   It's Caroline.

R4   She walks towards me.
Puts her fingers to my lips.
Puts her fingers inside my mouth.
I suck.
She smiles.

R3   Hello, slut.

R4   The woman on the bed sighs and stretches.
The naked woman pours the rest of the coke onto a compact.
She cuts three big lines.
She offers me the first.
She takes the second.
The sleeping woman takes the third.

R2   The coke hits me like metal.
I swig the remains of champagne.
I join them on the bed.

R1   Lick me.

R4   I lick.

R3   Suck me.

R2 I suck.

R1 Worship me.

R4 I worship her.

R3 Kiss my arse.

R2 And I know if I do so I will be lost.

R4 Is this a fantasy?

R1 Why do you ask?

R4 It feels so real.

R1 Perhaps it is.

R4 Am I crazy?

R2 Am I?

R4 Am I dead?

R3 Am I?

R2 Is she?

R1 And he?

R4 Did I?

R2 Am I Ray?

R4 Did I let the fire go out?
Did I pour water on the flames?
Did I boil my own skin?
Is that why I'm tormented by memories I can hardly
remember?

R2 I can see my father.
I'm in a field.
He's walking towards me.
He's smiling.
He holds out his hand.
I shake it.
He puts his arms around my shoulders.
I am his blood.

I am his son.
He makes me happy.
He'll never go away.
He loves me.
I love him.

Beat.

R4   She doesn't want to see you any more, Ray.
One day the pain will go away, Ray.
But you've got to give it time.

R2   Time.

R4   Be kind to yourself.

R2   Kind.

R4   Learn to love yourself.

R2   Love.

R4   Like I have.

Beat.

R2   I don't know if I can, Dad.

R4   Why not?

R2   I think I've been substituted.

R1   When I was asleep.

R3   By God.

R1   God did it.
Put someone else in my body instead of me.
Took me off.
Like in soccer.
I got substituted in the first half.
For no reason.
Wasn't I pulling my weight?
Or was it a tactical decision?
You took me off and put someone else on.
Instead of me.

Early bath.
Back to the dressing room.
Sitting with an anorak on.
What did I do wrong?
What the fuck did I do WRONG?
Did I shame you or something?
Did I?
Is there no remand?
No reprieve?
No reselection?
It's not me.
I look at a photograph.
Of the man I was.
In black and white.
That man is not me.

R2   You substituted me.
And all I want is
To get back on the pitch
You know what I'm saying?
Do I deserve this?
Is this what you want?
Is it? Is it?

R3   Where's Ray gone?
The old Ray? Real Ray.
Is he in this city?
Because crazy Ray is looking for him.

R2   Real Ray, you out there?
I been looking for you
You seen me?
I've written my number on your photograph, Ray,
And left them all over the city
Public places
No-star hotels
Urinals, chain stores and churches
Even nailed them into trees in the park
You seen him?

R1   I've followed trails that
Have led me nowhere.
I seen things I'd rather forget.
I been down blind alleys.
And to secret executions.

R3   I want you back, Ray.
And when I've got you back
Maybe she'll come back too.

R4   I want to be myself again
I want to open a window on a Sunday morning
And see her lying next to me
One small foot on top of the other
Asleep
Alive
She's come back to me
She's come home
Light floods into the house.

R1   Winter is behind us
The grass grows
Fish in ponds think of food for the first time in months
Starting a new cycle.

R4   Wipe away the dark.
The lies.
The disease.
The cancer.
I stand at the back door.
Listening to the ravens calling or rooks.

R2   There is light in my eyes.
There is love.

R4   I shave.
Put on a summer shirt.
Tidy up the house.
The remains of night.
The dust.
The waste.

R3   I am myself again . . . almost good.

R4   If the fish lasted the winter underwater without food
Surely so can I
Surely
Stop the infection.

R2   The disease.

R4   The addiction.

R1   The loathing.

R3   The self-hate.

R1   The destruction.

R4   The lies.

R1   The fabrication.

R2   The hate.
Because, even after everything I've done, I'm still loved.

Beat.

R3   Still.

R2   But did she ever really know me?

R1   Does he know me?

R3   Does he?

R1   Does he?

R4   Better than the voices.

R2   The demons.

R4   The shadows of the night that call.

R2   By phone.

R1   By image.

R3   By imagination.

R4   By desire.

R2   By lust.

R3   By my expectation.

R1   My anticipation.

R4   My addiction.

R2   Do the fish know?

R3   If I put my hand in the water will they eat?

R1   Would they rather starve than take food from me?

R4   I shiver with cold.
And now hear nothing.
No birdsong.
Or the screams of Sunday.

R2   I hear a distant siren.
And the rustle of a curtain against the paper.
The siren gets louder.
Are they coming for me?
Are they?
The Angels of Death.
Are they outside the door?

R4   I run upstairs to the bedroom.
She's not there.
Where is she?
WHERE THE FUCK IS SHE?

R1   There's blood on the walls.

R3   And on the streets.

R2   And on my hands.
What the fuck's happened here?

R1   This is not my house.

R3   This is not my home.

R4   Where the fuck am I? (*Beat.*)
This light
This summer shirt
Is an illusion.

R1   This is no garden party
Of Martini cocktails and dry white wine.

R2   This is a hotel room.

R4   I can't get the blood off my hands.
I scrub and scrub.

R2   Did I?

R3   Did you?

R4   Did I really murder my wife?

R2   Did I really put her in bin-liners
And put her in the rubbish?

R4   Like I did with the jewels of my soul? Did I?

R2   Did I watch from the shadows as the kitchen porter
dragged out the detritus of a busy night? Fish, flesh, fowl,
squid, hake.

R4   Did I watch him go towards the skip trolley? At the
back of the Continental?

R2   Did I hear the screams of the city
As the pubs chuck out and people
Fall into the streets of St Mary
And Womanby drowning?

R1   Did you?

R4   Did I watch as he opened the lid
Drop the rubbish
Freeze on the spot
As he sees a pair of beautiful blue eyes
Like glass.
Stare back at him?
Is that the face?
He keeps on seeing.
Over and over again.
Won't leave him.
A dead woman's face.
Looking back at him.
As if he did it?

R2   My wife.

R4   Did I do it?

R2   Or was it me?

R3   Or me?

R1   Or me?

Beat.

R4   I look out of the window.
Except for two loved-up ravers looking up at the clouds
Stoned
Mashed
Blue
The city is quiet.

R1   Maybe they know too
About the stone
The stone that started all this
That was thrown in the river
That created the commotion
It sank to the bottom
Took many years.

R2   It sank quietly, every fall reverberating against the
surface, making waves, ripples which turn into rings, every
moment of the stone's fall makes another circle, an echo, a
ring of what was once heard, a splash, something real, created,
heard, saw, beautiful, a possibility, the fish underneath heard
it, the birds of the air heard it, the animals of the field, the
planets round the sun, all heard it, even I heard it.
It happened. It did occur.

R3   I heard it too.

R1   Did I?

R4   Forefathers, ancestors, those who once were heard it.
They lived with it.

R2   Grew with it.

R4   Understood it.

R2   As a mystery.

R4   It gave them life.

R2   Helped them carry on through death, they made it.
Civilisation.

R4   They became colour and light and shade, they passed
on to their daughters and sons the news of what they heard.

R2   They made history.

R1   I thought I knew.
Could still see
Could still hear
The stone still falling
Silent in its underwater world
I thought it would fall for ever and while it fell through time
the rings around it would get bigger, wider, all-encompassing,
I would never forget, always remember.

R2   But then the stone stopped falling.

R3   Did it reach the bottom?

R4   Did it come to an end?

R2   Did it send out a siren, a distress call that it was falling
no more?

R3   Did it send out its last signal?

R3   Its last reverberation?
The last cycle?
The last ring?
Is that why the river that lies before me is silent?
Is still.
Is that why I see people gather in droves to stare at the sea?
Have they come to hear
The last echo of history?
Does their memory fail them?
Have they forgotten to remember?
Or did we remember to forget?

Is that why I stand afraid
On the shores of the still river?

R4   Alone.

R1   Terrified.

R3   Without meaning?

R1   No direction.

R4   The home I once knew.

R1   Lost.

R4   Where am I?

R1   It's just a hotel room.

R4   Nothing special.

R3   Corporate.

R4   Anonymous.

R1   Functional.

R2   I am alone.

R4   Me too.

R4   And me.

R2   Who stands in this silence?

R1   If the stone hit the bottom
Then I will hear no more.

R4   I will be stone dead.

R1   I may hope that the stone is suspended.

R2   In limbo.

R4   In a current.

R3   A whirlpool.

R4   Temporarily spinning.

R1   But that it will one day.

R4   Spin free.

R2   In a flurry.

R4   Of light.

R3   And weight.

R4   And will continue its falling.

R1   Down, down, on its infinite path.

R2   So that I may hear the commotion again –

R3   The life rising from deep –

R1   To the surface of the river –

R2   The still river –

R4   And the cycle will grow –

R3   The ring expand –

R2   I may hear again –

R4   See again –

R1   Know again –

R2   Remember again –

R4   Love again –

R1   Never forget –

R2   The things I once knew –

R4   I could almost touch –

R3   The skin of light –

R1   The warmth of blood –

R4   The things I thought lost –

R2   In the still river of time.

Beat.

R4   Fuck.

R2   Fuck.

R1   Fuck.

R3   Fuck.

R4   Has my story come to an end?

R1   Am I home?

R2   Is home –

R4   Or my idea of home –

R1   Which I've carried around in my head –

R3   And in my heart –

R4   Like a memory –

R1   Like the corpse of a still-born child –

R2   No more than a womb for the dead . . .?

R3   Gone?

R1   Erased?

R2   Forever?

R4   If it is . . . what's left?

Silence.

R1   Just a story.

R2   With no one around to listen to.

R3   Fragments.

R2   Bits and pieces.

R1   Words.

R4   Pictures.

R3   Meaning nothing.

R4   All the things I thought we'd do.

R1   Should have done.

R2   Should have but didn't.

R3   Possibilities.

R2   Things hoped for.

R1   Yearned for.

R4   Loved for.

R2   To be forgiven for.

R1   Not killed for.

R3   Or hated for.

R2   Not blamed.

R4   But been.

R1   Been.

R3   Been.

R1   Has it all been for nothing?

R4   Am I alone?

R2   Us myself. Myself and us.

R1   The stories I know.

R4   And the stories I don't.

R1   In my head.

R2   Your head.

R4   Our head ourselves.

R2   Myself us.

R1   Who would have said –

R4   Not me.

R3   Or me.

R4   Who would have thought –

R1   Not me.

R2   Or me.

R4   That it would come to this.

Beat.

Hello?
Hello?
Hello?

Beat.

R1   It's morning.

R2   It's me.

R3   I know.

R4   I love you.

End.